"Comfort, Comfort My People...."

A course on Jewish/Christian relations

By George Hans Liebenow

Study Guide

Revised Edition

Edited by the Staff of the Board for Parish Services
Editor: Earl H. Gaulke

Produced cooperatively with the Task Force on Witnessing to Jewish People
of the Board for Mission Services
The Lutheran Church—Missouri Synod

Copyright © 1979, 1991 Concordia Publishing House
3558 South Jefferson Avenue
St. Louis, MO 63118-3968
Manufactured in the United States of America

Cover photo by H. Armstrong Roberts.

Unless otherwise indicated, Scripture quotations are from the Revised Standard Version of
the Bible, copyrighted 1946, 1952, © 1971, 1973. Used by permission.

The Scripture quotation marked Phillips is from J. B. Phillips: THE NEW TESTAMENT IN
MODERN ENGLISH Revised Edition © J. B. Phillips 1958, 1960, 1972. Used by permission of MacMillan Publishing Co., Inc.

Contents

Foreword: Aim of the Course

Out of the world's population of five billion people, there are only about 16 million Jews today, considerably less than one percent of the total. Yet, Jewish influence and contributions to a vast array of arts, sciences, letters, business, and finance far exceed their numbers. Who does not know the names of these prominent Jewish people: statesmen Henry Kissinger, Arthur Goldberg, and Abba Eban? world-renowned scientists Jonas Salk and Albert Einstein? theologians Abraham Heschel and Elie Wiesel? astronaut Judith Resnik? violinists Jascha Heifetz, Isaac Stern, and Itzhak Perlman? composers George Gershwin, Irving Berlin, Leonard Bernstein, and Sammy Cahn? pianists Artur Rubinstein, and Vladimir Horowitz? performers Victor Borge, Bob Dylan, Jack Benny, Paul Newman, Barbra Streisand, Kirk Douglas, and many others, all of whom are household names? dramatist Arthur Miller? novelists Saul Bellow and Herman Wouk? The list is indeed long, and their accomplishments range over a wide field of human endeavor.

Who are these people, the Jews? What do modern Jews have in common with the ancient Jews we read about in the Bible? And what about the modern state of Israel? Most important of all: What *relationship* is there—and can there be—between Jews and Christians?

All these questions—and many more—will be addressed in the course you're about to begin. More specifically, the course aims to help you do the following:

1. Recognize Jewish people as people. They, like we, were created by the Father (**Acts 17:26**) and reconciled through the Son (**2 Corinthians 5:19**). They too are included in the "all men" whom God the Holy Spirit would lead "to be saved and to come to the knowledge of the truth" in Jesus (**1 Timothy 2:4**).

2. Love them.
3. Understand their thinking about religion and their history—including the history of Christian persecution of Jews.
4. Better appreciate and receive the blessings of God's love given through the Jews **(John 4:22).**
5. Be enabled to share with them—in love—the Gospel message: "In Christ Jesus you are all sons of God, through faith. . . . There is neither Jew nor Greek . . . for you are all one in Christ Jesus" **(Galatians 3:26–28).**

1. Who Are the Jews?

The Aim of This Session

1. To learn the meaning of biblical, historical, and modern terms that refer to Jews.
2. To grow in understanding and appreciation of God's grace in calling out for Himself a chosen people—in Old Testament times and today.

Abraham, the Forebear of the Jews

Although the word often translated "Jew" doesn't appear in the Bible until Jeremiah's time, the Jews of today (and also of Jesus' day) claim Abraham as their forebear.

1. What do you remember about Abraham? (Share Bible stories you remember.)
2. Read **Genesis 12:1–3** and **Acts 7:2–8.** What do these texts say about the claim that Abraham was the forebear of the Jews?

Descendants of Abraham

1. **Acts 7:8** lists the immediate descendants of Abraham. Who were they?
2. Compare the promises given to Abraham (**Genesis 12:1–3, 7**) with the promises given to his descendants: **Genesis 26:1–4; 28:10–14; 35:9–12.** On the basis of these texts, is it correct to say that the Jews are descendants of Abraham, Isaac, and Jacob?

People of the Covenant

A covenant is a promise or agreement entered into by two or more parties. In ancient times a covenant was "signed" or sealed, usually in the presence of witnesses, with oaths and religious rites. (In **Genesis 21:25–32** a covenant settled an argument about a well. In **2 Samuel 3:12–21** the adoption of a covenant between Abner and David ended a civil war and assured support for David as king.)

God initiated various covenants with His people. What covenant did He establish with Noah **(Genesis 9:9–11)**?

The covenant with Noah is a universal covenant, and it pertains to all humanity. But as God began to choose for Himself a special, a peculiar people, He made specific covenants with Abraham and his descendants. So we can properly call Abraham and his descendants "people of the covenant." (You can read more about God's covenants with Abraham and his descendants in **Genesis 15:18** and **17:1–14.**)

A few hundred years later, when God led His people out of Egypt to Mount Sinai, He inaugurated another covenant, which is often referred to as the mosaic covenant. Its circumstances, conditions, and ratification are recorded in **Exodus 19–24.** Scan these chapters quickly. Did God make this covenant with all peoples, or just with Israel? Which most important part of the covenant is in **Exodus 20?**

In **2 Samuel 7** we see that God established a covenant with David. In **Jeremiah 31:31–34** the Lord promised to make a new covenant with the house of Israel and the house of Judah. What is this Jeremiah text referring to? (Note the importance of forgiveness of sin **[31:34].**) Compare this passage with **1 Corinthians 11:23–26.**

Israel

Abraham's son of promise was Isaac, and Isaac's son of promise was Jacob. Do you recall the Bible narratives about Jacob and Esau's family quarrel? (Share what you remember.) When Jacob was on his way home from his uncle Laban's, the angel of the Lord wrestled with Jacob and changed his name to *Israel,* which means "He who strives with God" or "God strives" **(Genesis 32:28).**

Jacob had a large family, including 12 sons. They and their progeny came to be known as the *B'ne Israel,* "the people of Israel." Since it was through the offspring of Isaac and Jacob (Israel) that God's promises to Abraham were fulfilled, we can refer to their descendants as "Israel."

Hebrew

In the Old Testament the word *Hebrew* comes from *Eber,* who was an ancestor of Abraham, and is used to refer to his descendants (see **Genesis 10:21–25; 11:14–26**). In the Ancient Near East a similar word was associated with a class of people, like laborers who served as merchants or caravanners. It often seems to have been used in a derogatory sense.

In the New Testament *Hebrew* is used 14 times; 10 times it refers to the Hebrew language. In **Acts 6:1** Hebrews are contrasted with Hellenists, but here too the reference is to language and culture.

In **2 Corinthians 11:22** St. Paul wrote: "Are they Hebrews? So am I. Are they Israelites? So am I. Are they descendants of Abraham? So am I." Evidently Paul wanted to show his Jewishness here, and he seems to have used a gradation of the various terms, possibly for dramatic or literary effect. The same seems to apply to Paul's statements in **Philippians 3:5.**

Jew

In the Bible the word translated as "Jew" or "Judahite" is relatively late. This Hebrew word, *Yehudi,* is derived from the name *Judah,* and its first biblical use is in the exilic and post-exilic periods. The one nation, Israel, split after Solomon's time into two nations. One of the new nations, in the northern part of the old Israel, continued to be called Israel. Composed of 10 tribes, it was conquered by the Assyrians in 721 B.C. The 10 tribes were taken into captivity, intermarried with foreigners, and so disappeared as a separate nation and people.

The Southern Kingdom, composed of the small tribe of Benjamin and the much larger tribe of Judah, was called the Kingdom of Judah. This nation, too, fell in time—to the Babylonians in 586 B.C. But most of its people, taken into captivity, did not intermarry with foreigners, and so they survived as a people. The term *Jew,* derived from *Judah,* thus refers, strictly speaking, to descendants of only two of the original 12 tribes of Israel.

In the New Testament, *Jew* is generally equated with the physical descendants of Abraham, Isaac, and Jacob. However, as St. Paul made a distinction between the physical descendants of Abraham and his spiritual descendants in **Galatians 3,** so in **Romans 2** he made the same distinction between Jews. See **Romans 2:28–29.**

Romans 4 emphasizes that Abraham is the "father of all who believe" **(4:11)**—both circumcised and uncircumcised. God's chosen people, in the deepest and truest sense of that phrase, are those who today, as in Old Testament times, share Abraham's faith in the God who forgives through His Son.

Summary

Having considered the various terms that refer to Jews, we can say that Abraham received the first spiritual promises that referred to a chosen people. The descendants of Abraham, Isaac, and Jacob were "people of the covenant." The covenant continued through Jacob, whose name was changed to Israel, and he was the progenitor of the 12 tribes of Israel and also of the nation called "Israel."

Generally, the descendants of Abraham, Isaac, and Jacob (Israel) are equated with "the people of Israel," or more simply "Israelites," or collectively "Israel." The term *Jew* dates from the time of the exile and derives from *Judah,* one of the two tribes remaining of the original 12. *Jew* in the New Testament and today is generally used as a synonym for "descendant of Abraham, Isaac, and Jacob," "person of Israel," or "Israelite."

Most important, regarding our relationship with God: "In Christ Jesus you are all sons of God, through faith. . . . There is neither Jew nor Greek; . . . you are all one in Christ Jesus. And if you are Christ's, then you are Abraham's offspring, heirs according to the promise" **(Galatians 3:26–29).** The Christian, whether Jew or Gentile, is Abraham's spiritual offspring.

For Discussion

1. What was most significant (interesting, important) for you in this lesson? Why?
2. Of the terms for the Jews studied in this lesson, what is the most *meaningful* one in your opinion? Why?

3. How did you feel the last time you talked to a Jewish person? What did you talk about? If you could talk with the same person now that you've finished this lesson, would your conversation be different? If so, how?
4. How did you feel the last time you talked *about* a Jewish person? Why? What was the conversation about? If you could have that conversation over again now, what do you hope would happen?

2. The Jews: A Short History

The Aim of This Session

1. To gain a better understanding of modern Jews through a brief study of their history.
2. To uncover and repent of any latent seeds of prejudice against Jews, and yield more fully to God's forgiving and enabling love in Christ for all people.

Return from Exile

Session 1 reviewed some of the history of God's dealing with His people in Old Testament times—up to the time of the Babylonian captivity. Jeremiah prophesied that this exile of the people of Judah would last 70 years. Although the city of Jerusalem was destroyed by the Babylonians in 586 B.C., some of the people of Judah were carried into exile beginning in 605. The first group of exiles returned to Judah in 538, almost 70 years later. They began rebuilding the temple in 536 and finally finished it in 516.

Some Jews remained in the lands where they had been settled, but a second group returned to Judah under Ezra (probably in 458). Ezra led the returnees in spiritual reform. The last group of exiles returned in 432 under Nehemiah. It was under Nehemiah that the returning exiles rebuilt the walls of Jerusalem.

If time permits, share Bible stories you remember about Ezra, Nehemiah, and their efforts. Or scan the two biblical books of Ezra and Nehemiah. What messages does God speak to us today through these books?

Intertestamental Period

Even though the last books of the Old Testament were completed some 300 years before the birth of Christ, we still know much about the history of the Jews during the intertestamental period from books called the Apocrypha, and also from secular historians. Many Jews began to settle in communities outside of Palestine (note, for example, the places mentioned in **Acts 2:1–11**). It was probably in the fifth or fourth century B.C. that Jews in the diaspora (Jews living in foreign countries) developed the synagogue. Here prayer and study took the place of temple worship, with its emphasis on animal sacrifice. Most likely it was also at this time that scribes (Bible scholars) promoted the intensive study and interpretation of the Scriptures. Jews rose to prominent positions in numerous governmental offices.

In the third century B.C. there were so many Jews in Alexandria, Egypt, who had forgotten the Hebrew language that their sacred writings had to be translated into Greek, and so the Septuagint was produced. This Greek translation of the Old Testament was much used also in early New Testament times.

Beginning at the time of Alexander the Great (who ruled from 336 to 323 B.C.), Greek philosophy, Greek culture, and the Greek language spread over the Mediterranean world, including Israel, and threatened the very life of traditional Judaism. In Israel the integration of Hellenism (Greek culture and philosophy) into Jewish life was radically implemented by Antiochus IV (Epiphanes) of Syria (175–164 B.C.). He not only promoted the pagan spirit of Hellenism but also persecuted the Jews who worshiped the one true God. (The history of this period is recorded in two of the apocryphal, or deuterocanonical, books—the First and Second Books of Maccabees.) Antiochus robbed the temple and set up a statue of Zeus in the holy of holies. He ordered that swine be sacrificed in the temple—a shocking desecration!

These outrages inspired the Jews to revolt. Mattathias and his sons, especially Judas Maccabaeus, led small bands of guerrilla fighters against the mighty Syrian armies and recaptured the Jerusalem temple compound. Judas rededicated the temple on the 25th of Chislev, 164 B.C. Since that time this event has been observed as Hanukkah, or the Feast of Lights. (The feast is mentioned in **John 10:22**.) A comprehensive Bible study guide on Hanukkah is available through the Task Force on Witnessing to Jewish People. Contact the Board for Mission Services, LCMS, 1333 S.

Kirkwood Road, St. Louis, MO 63122-7295, Attention: Chairman, Task Force on Witnessing to Jewish People.

In 63 B.C. the conquering Romans, under Pompey, came to Syro-Palestine and helped the family of Antipater (an Idumean, or Edomite, not Jewish) to rule the Holy Land. Herod, named the Great, son of Antipater, was king when Jesus was born in Bethlehem.

1. Although the events recorded in the book of Esther occurred shortly before Ezra's return to Jerusalem, they relate the origin of another still-celebrated Jewish festival—Purim. Review what you remember from the book of Esther. Read **Esther 9:16–28.** What message do you think the book of Esther has for Christians today? for Jews?
2. What meaning(s) might you as a Christian find in the victory that Jews celebrate on Hanukkah?

Through the Middle Ages

In A.D. 70 a Roman army under Titus crushed a Jewish revolt and destroyed the temple in Jerusalem. Thus ended the era of temple sacrifice. Forcefully expelled from their holy city of Jerusalem (as many as 100,000 Jewish captives were taken to Rome), the Jewish dispersion among the nations increased. Most of the last remnant of the political Jewish rebels—a group of 960—committed suicide at the fortress of Masada in A.D. 73 rather than be captured by the Romans.

After A.D. 70, Babylonia (modern Iraq) became the seat of Judaic learning. The most authoritative edition of the Talmud was completed there in the fifth century A.D. This edition consists of 63 books of legal, ethical, and historical writings—all of which grew out of rabbinical interpretations of the Jewish Bible (the Old Testament).

In the seventh century A.D. both the mideastern and western worlds were changed by the rise of Islam, the religion of Muhammad. Muslims, as adherents of this religion are called, consider themselves the true spiritual descendants of Abraham. They honor Jesus as a prophet but do not believe in His deity. The followers of Muhammad conquered the entire Middle East, as well as Egypt and the rest of northern Africa; even Spain fell under Muslim influence. During this period many Jews continued to migrate to Europe. Christianity had been firmly embedded there, and Jews were consistently treated as a minority group.

In 1099 the Roman Catholic Church launched the first of its crusades—allegedly to save the Holy Land from the "infidel" Muslims. The crusades will forever be a blot on the Christian Church. The term *crusade* is derived from the Latin word *crux,* cross. Our Lord Jesus Christ said: "If any man would come after Me, let him deny himself and take up his cross and follow Me" **(Matthew 16:24).** But the church's crusaders picked up the sword and ravaged the land in a way that is still not forgotten by Muslims, nor by Jews.

But the brutality of the crusaders did little to lessen either the zeal or the numbers of Muslims. In fact, the followers of Muhammad soon regained control of the Holy Land and continued as cultural masters as far as Spain. Meanwhile, Jews continued to migrate to most European cities, and many assumed prominent positions as teachers, doctors, and advisers to political courts.

But during this period many Jews were also persecuted by Christians. England was the last country to admit Jews and the first to drive them out, beginning in 1215. In France, Jews were expelled under Louis IX (1226–70) and Philip the Fair (1285–1314). There was no mass expulsion from Germany, but local governments regularly conducted pogroms (organized massacres), causing Jews to keep on the move. The greatest expulsion took place in Spain in 1492.

During the period of the late Middle Ages and during the Protestant Reformation, Italy and Germany had large Jewish populations. Sometimes the Jews lived under benign rulers like popes Leo X (1513–21) and Clement VII (1522–34). At the same time there were some churchmen like Martin Luther who, though originally friendly to the Jews because he hoped for their inclusion into the church, later called for harsh treatment of them, including confiscating their money and depriving them of their civil rights.

The expulsion of Jews from Spain swelled the Jewish population of the Turkish Ottoman Empire. Persecuted Jews from England, France, and Germany fled to Poland, which counted about half a million Jews in 1650. Today the majority of world Jewry is descended from this latter segment.

1. Read **Luke 19:41–44.** What event does Jesus here predict? What is it that brings God's eventual judgment on people—then and now? What

in this text emphasizes God's love for sinners? Why would it be a *misuse* and *misreading* of this text to use it as a justification for hating modern Jews?

2. Read **Matthew 16:21–27; 26:50–53.** What do these texts have to say about the church's motivation in the crusades? about the way we can best "defend" our Christian faith—and share it with Jews and/or other non-Christian groups or individuals?

Jews in the New World

In the ghettos of Europe, Jewish life continued with difficulty. With the coming of the so-called "Age of Enlightenment" in the 18th century, Jews detected a ray of hope. Here and there some Jews were well received and some even served in high government positions. Emigration to the New World gave great hope to the Jews. Many thousands came to the United States and Canada, until by 1914 their numbers reached about four million in the U.S.A. alone. Today there are more than six million Jews in the United States.

U.S. and Canadian Jewry is generally urban, with about 30 percent of U.S. Jews living in the greater New York City area. That makes two million, which equals two-thirds of the Jewish population of the state of Israel! Most Jews live somewhat in proximity to each other, so it's possible for them to continue serving conveniently in Jewish affairs, as in local temples and synagogues, in fraternal services, and in community programs.

Demographic studies show that Jews, like other Americans, generally move to the suburbs. For example, in 1958 in Cleveland, Ohio, 85 percent of its Jews lived beyond that city's boundaries. About 80 percent of Jewish college-age youth are enrolled in higher-education institutions. So it follows that there is a greater percentage of Jews that are engaged in professional occupations.

During the 1950s and 1960s there was a general religious revival in the United States and Canada. Judaism too experienced an increased interest and growth in religious affairs, although Jewish attendance at public worship remains relatively low. (We must remember, however, that Jewish religious life to a great extent centers in the home.) The formation of the state of Israel on May 14, 1948, had much to do with the revival of the spirit of Jewishness.

Because the state of Israel is a Jewish nation and the original home of their ancestors and because it has offered a haven and a homeland for Jews from all over the world, many U.S. Jews have a profound interest in and a special relationship with Israel. Some U.S. and Canadian Jews have emigrated to Israel, although a number of these have returned. But loans and gifts from the United States help keep the shaky Israeli economy going. Before and after the June 1967 war, Jews raised $75,000,000 for Israel in bonds and contributed $232,000,000 to the United Jewish Appeal. (Jews are very generous givers to other charities too.)

Generally, our Jewish friends have enjoyed more freedom and less discrimination in Canada and the United States than in almost any other part of the world throughout history. But the record is not perfect. Silent and subtle discrimination is promoted by clubs closed to Jews, by enrollment quotas at certain schools, and by discrimination in housing. Periodically, crass anti-Semitism raises its ugly head through publications like *The Cross and the Flag* and *Common Sense* and through organizations like the American Nazi Party and the National Renaissance Party.

The Holocaust

Undoubtedly the most vicious attack on the Jews was the systematic persecution and mass murder that European Jews suffered under Adolf Hitler's Nazi dictatorship. Of the estimated 12 million people executed by the Nazis (not counting those killed in actual warfare), as many as six million were Jews—more than a third of the total Jewish world population.

Some Christians in Germany spoke out against Nazi persecution of the Jews. Pastor Martin Niemoeller, in his last sermon to his Christian congregation, encouraged them: "We must obey God rather than men." But he was arrested and put into a concentration camp. Thousands of other pastors and Christian laypeople were imprisoned and executed.

But sad to say, many people who called themselves Christians helped the Nazis, or at least closed their eyes to the Nazi persecution of the Jews—not only in Germany, but in the rest of Europe and the Western Hemisphere. Immigration laws in the U.S. and other countries kept out many Jews who might otherwise have escaped persecution.

1. Share your recollections of—and your feelings about—any movies, T.V. documentaries, or books about the holocaust, for example, *The Diary of Anne Frank.*
2. "The Jews crucified Christ. They deserved what they got in the holocaust." Is this kind of sentiment really justified by **Matthew 27:25,** as some Christians have claimed? See **Acts 4:23–28; Romans 9:2–3.** Who is it, really, who crucified Jesus?
3. Share your reaction to the following statement, said to have been made by Pastor Martin Niemoeller:

> *First the Nazis came for the Communists; and I didn't speak up because I wasn't a Communist. Then they came for the Jews; and I didn't speak up because I wasn't a Jew. When they came for the trade unionists I didn't speak up, because I wasn't a trade unionist. And when they came for the Catholics I didn't speak up, because I was a Protestant. Then they came for me . . . and by that time there was no one left to speak for anyone.*

For Further Discussion

1. What impresses you most about the history of the Jews?
2. In what respects is the history of Jews different from that of other groups of people?
3. Why do you suppose Jews have been persecuted so often?
4. Name one thing that you pray God will enable you to do as a result of this lesson.

". . . a light for revelation to the Gentiles, and for glory to Thy people Israel." Luke 2:22–32

3. *Common Roots*

The Aim of This Session

1. To affirm the common roots of the Christian and Jewish religious communities in the Old Testament.
2. While recognizing differences, to highlight common teachings and practices.
3. To review the roots of the teachings of Jesus in the history and Scriptures of Judaism.

Back to Basics

Both Christians and Jews accept the books of the Bible called the Old Testament by Christians (and the Tanak by Jews) as God's revealed Word. The Hebrew Bible, the basic religious document of the Jews, makes up more than two-thirds of the Christian Scriptures.

But while it is true that the Old Testament is fundamental to both faiths, both also have sacred writings that differ.

The Christian community has the New Testament, seen as the necessary completion of the Old, a revelation that presents Jesus as Messiah and Savior and is, for that reason, the climax of the life and faith of Israel and the fulfillment of Old Testament prophecy and promise.

The Jewish community has the Talmud as additional sacred writings derived from the Old Testament and developed through tradition.

Religious practice and beliefs in the Jewish community today differ radically from those of Bible times. Jews no longer worship in the Jerusalem temple, nor do they sacrifice animals as prescribed in the Hebrew Scriptures. Much of Jewish faith-life today is based on the Talmud, a massive collection of writings composed by rabbis through the centuries that serves as a comment on and expansion of the core religious teachings of the Old Testament.

The Talmud is divided into two parts. The Mishnah, collected as a body of writings about A.D. 200, contains explanations of and comment on laws about agriculture, feasts, fasts, marriage, civil law, criminal law, and the like. Much of the material in the Mishnah probably goes back to Jesus' time. The Gemara serves as a commentary on the Mishnah and an expansion of it.

The Talmud is not just laws and more laws. Though it explains and particularizes the law, much of it is in the form of parable and dialog. Read this parable:

> *Once when I was on a journey, I came upon a man who went at me after the manner of the heretics. Now, he accepted the written but not the oral law. He said to me: "The written law was given us from Mount Sinai; the oral law was not given us from Mount Sinai." I said to him: "But were not both the Written and the Oral Law spoken by the Omnipresent? Then what difference is there between the written and the oral law?"*
>
> *To what can this (case) be compared? To a king of flesh and blood who had two servants, and loved them both with a perfect love. One day he gave them each a measure of wheat, and each a bundle of flax.*
>
> *The wise servant, what did he do? He took the flax and spun a cloth. Then he took the wheat and made flour. He cleansed the flour, ground, kneaded and baked it, and set it on a table. Then he spread the cloth over it and so left it until the king should return.*
>
> *But the foolish servant? He did nothing at all. After some days the king returned from his journey and came into his house and said to his servants: "My sons, bring me what I gave you."*
>
> *The first servant showed the wheat bread on the table with the cloth spread over it. The other servant showed the wheat still in the box, with a bundle of flax upon it. Alas for his shame! Alas for his disgrace!*

Now when the Holy One, blessed be He, gave the Torah to Israel, He gave it only in the form of wheat, for us to extract flour from it, and flax to extract a garment (Seder Eliyahu Zutta II).

What does this parable say about the attitude of some Jews toward the tradition of the rabbis? What parable of Jesus does this selection remind you of? Would Jesus have agreed with this selection? Why or why not?

Jesus the Rabbi

Though Jews and Christians share a common core of Scripture in the Old Testament, the emphasis of each community on their unique written revelation (the New Testament and the Talmud) would tend to increase separation. But even these are not entirely exclusive.

The differences between Jew and Christian represented in their religious writings were not so apparent when Jesus began His ministry. Jesus did not, indeed, come to establish a new religion but to fulfill the Law and the prophets. As a Jewish rabbi, or teacher, "He went about all Galilee, teaching in their synagogues" **(Matthew 4:23)**. Jesus was recognized as "a teacher . . . from God" **(John 3:2)** because of His miracles and His prophetic words. Jesus taught about some subjects that were also of concern to other Jewish rabbis.

1. Look up some of these passages and compare them to the words of the Talmud quoted below: **Matthew 6:25–26, 30, 34; 7:7; 5:28;** and **Luke 6:38.**

   "As you open your hand to the poor, so others shall open to you" (Midrash Tannaim 15:8).

   "He who says 'What shall I eat tomorrow?' lacks faith, for it is said, 'The day's lot is in its day' " (Mekilta 16:4).

   "Seek and find the place the Lord your God will choose" (Sifre on Deut. 12:5).

   "The eye: lest you should think only he who sins with his body is an adulterer. He who sins with his eye is also an adulterer" (Ahare Mot 23:12).

   "Did you ever see an animal or bird that had a trade? Yet they support themselves without trouble. Does it not follow that I shall be supported without trouble?" (Kiddushin 4:14).

Even though some of Jesus' teachings were similar to some Jewish oral teachings, He strongly denounced those traditions that "made void the Word of God" (**Matthew 15:6**). Read **Matthew 15:1–14 (Mark 7:1–13); Matthew 23:16–22.** It was in part because He rejected so many of the traditions of the rabbis that the religious leaders of His day finally planned to kill Him (**Matthew 26:3–4; Luke 22:2; John 11:45–53**).

2. Jesus' perfect prayer is a thoroughly Jewish prayer, which flows from Old Testament teaching. As such, some of its petitions were echoed in the teachings of some of the rabbis.

   Compare the following:

   "Let Thy great name be magnified and hallowed" (The Kaddish).

   "Do Thy will in the heavens above and give tranquility of spirit to those who fear Thee on earth" (Berakoth T 3.7).

   "Lead us not into temptation, but keep us far from all evil" (Beer. 16b).

3. Read again His encounter with Nicodemus in **John 3:1–21.** Why does Nicodemus approach Jesus with such reverence? What service did he provide later? See **John 19:38–42.** Why? List the crucial differences in Jesus' teaching that set Him apart from other rabbis.

4. It is important to note that Nicodemus was a Pharisee. In His teaching, Jesus supported many of the convictions of the Pharisees: heaven, hell, angels, devils, the Last Judgment, and the like. The Sadducees opposed those teachings. How might that help explain the violence of their hatred of Jesus? See **Luke 22:2.** (In Jesus' day most chief priests were Sadducees and many scribes, or teachers of the law, were Pharisees.) What was the attitude of the common people?

Early Christianity

1. It was a Pharisee who was still open to the possibility that Jesus was indeed "from God." What does Gamaliel say in **Acts 5:33–39?** How did he view Jesus and His followers?

   Often we characterize the growth of the early church as the spread of a religion "new" to Jews and Gentiles alike. We see Paul as the proponent of a "new" Gospel and the Christians as completely separate from their Jewish roots. That is far from the case. It is true that it was a difficult struggle for some to come to terms with Jewish traditions in the Christian community, but the view that some Christians were trying to put Jewish elements into early Christian practice is the reverse of reality. Actually, early Jewish believers saw their acceptance of Jesus as Messiah as a part of their Jewish faith. They were simply reluctant to reject the many laws and rules that had been a part of their religious practice. They insisted on circumcision and obedience to Old Testament law as natural for those who had completed their Jewish faith by accepting Jesus as Messiah.

2. Scan the account of the confrontation at Jerusalem between the "Judaizers" and Paul in **Acts 15.** What insight into the conflict and resolution can you gain from remembering that Peter and his friends were devout Jews trying to deal with their traditional religious practice?

Many of Paul's writings to the churches (e.g., Romans, Galatians, Colossians) deal with the issue of the insistence by some Jewish Christians that observance of ceremonial laws was necessary to Christian faith and faith-life. Paul rejects that position **(Colossians 2:16–17; Galatians 2:11–16)** but interestingly, not his Jewishness. How does he view his relationship to the Jews? See **2 Corinthians 11:22; Romans 4:1; 9:1–5.**

Roots Rejected

As early as the second century there was a move in the church to rid Christianity of everything Jewish. A false teacher named Marcion attempted to set the Old and New Covenants at odds and declare that the faith and practice of the Old Testament was flawed. He felt that God was portrayed in a distorted way in the Old Testament as a vengeful and angry despot and that only in the New Testament could the great God of the universe be known. Though Marcion was eventually excommunicated for his false teaching, much of what he brought into the Christian religion carried on through the ages. Even today attitudes remain that conclude that the Old Testament is all law, that it is just background for the New

Testament, that it presents a clouded picture of God, and that it contains a flawed, legalistic covenant. How would you respond to those who claim that the Old Testament is distorted, legalistic, and unnecessary? What does that kind of opinion say about Jesus as the promised Messiah?

In Common—And Different

In spite of the common roots there are important differences between Jews and Christians. Many of these differences center on the Christian claim that Jesus Christ is the Son of God, true God, and the Savior of the world. This basic tenet of Christianity is rejected by Jews. Moreover, Jewish people (other than Jewish Christians) believe that atonement with God happens because of their works of law (deeds) rather than just by faith. Nevertheless, commonalties abound.

Here is a partial list of some of the teachings and practices that Jews and Christians share: the oneness of God, God as Creator, the Ten Commandments, the Tanak (Old Testament), worship in a "temple," worship at an altar, worship as thanksgiving and praise, worship on a select day of the week, responsive prayers, prayers for the people, tithes, worship with musical instruments, chants, hymns, the reading of Scripture in worship, the home as a central unit of worship. Can you list others? Remember, Martin Luther wrote: "The Old Testament is the cradle into which God placed His Son."

What differences can you list between Jews and Christians?

For Discussion

1. What was most significant (important, interesting) in this lesson for you? Why?
2. What is the best way to affirm the common roots that Jews and Christian share?

4. Jews Today

The Aim of This Session

1. To understand the teachings and philosophy of the Jewish community today, particularly in North America.
2. To look at some of the current and historic movements in Judaism.
3. To glimpse what it means to live as a Jew in North America.

What Makes a Person a Jew?

This question is not as easy to answer as it might appear. Judaism is a religion, but many who are Jews by birth hold none of the tenets of traditional Judaism. Some consider Jewry to be a culture, an ethnic way of living, but in many countries Jews have almost completely adopted the lifestyle and culture of their host nations. Some claim that Jews are a race and Jewishness is inherited, but converts to Judaism do not necessarily come from Semitic stock.

Who are the Jews then? What makes a person a Jew? Basically Jews are people who consider themselves Jews, regardless of religious conviction, practice, lifestyle, or bloodline.

And it is because modern Judaism has become such a huge, inclusive umbrella that it is difficult to determine just what it is that Jews believe.

In very recent times, the official position of the State of Israel on what legally constitutes a Jew was codified. That definition says that a person is a Jew who was born of a Jewish mother or who has undergone conversion through the supervision of an orthodox rabbi. The most noteworthy action taken by the Israeli parliament (Knesset) was to declare that a person who would qualify for immediate Israeli citizenship under the Law of Return would not be granted such citizenship if he or she were a professing believer in Jesus Christ as Lord and Savior.

Judaism as a Religion

To the extent that Judaism has teachings about God and humans, a system of ethics, traditions, and ritual, it is a religion. But there is great diversity of belief and practice in the Jewish community.

Basically, in the U.S. and Canada, there are three forms of Judaism: Orthodox, Reform, and Conservative. But these are descriptive groupings rather than finely delineated denominations. Some people consider themselves as part of more than one of the segments while others (e.g., Hasidic Jews) don't want to be part of any of them.

But for all three of the above expressions of Judaism, the core of religious teachings is the *Shema*: "Hear, O Israel: The Lord our God is one Lord" **(Deuteronomy 6:4)**.

The Three Divisions

1. Orthodox Judaism

The Orthodox are religious Jews who believe that the Torah, both the written Torah (Genesis–Deuteronomy) and the oral Torah (the Mishnah), is the inspired Word of God and that they fulfill their Jewish heritage and live in relationship to God as they obey the laws and teachings of the Tanak (Old Testament) and sacred tradition. They carefully observe the sabbath laws, the injunctions of the Talmud, and observe all the traditional feasts and festivals. They abide by the strict dietary rules in Exodus and Leviticus as literally as possible in the 20th century. While the exact number of Jews following orthodox beliefs and practices is unknown, it is generally accepted that a very small number of Jewish people (possibly as few as 10 percent in North America) consider themselves Orthodox and hold membership in Orthodox synagogues. A survey taken by the Jewish Federation Council of Greater Los Angeles revealed that only five percent of Jewish people in that city identified themselves as Orthodox.

Scan **Leviticus 11.** What practical reasons for the laws do you see? How would the prohibitions have helped the Hebrews of Moses' time?

What difficulties do you see in trying to observe those dietary regulations today?

2. Reform Judaism

First a movement in 19th-century Europe, Reform Judaism was popularized in North America by Rabbi Isaac Mayer Wise. Reform Judaism is rationalistic, liberal Judaism. To the Reform Jew the Hebrew Scriptures are developments of the Jewish people and not divine revelation and the writings of the Talmud are historical commentaries rather than rules to live by. Reform Judaism is basically an ethical society affirming the fatherhood of God and the brotherhood of humankind. Most Reform Jews consider the mission of Judaism to work toward reformation and moralization of society and the eventual realization of a peaceful and just civilization.

Here is a statement contained in literature distributed by the National Conference of Christians and Jews and affirmed by many Reform Jews:

> *We believe in one God, Creator and Sustainer of the Universe. . . . we hold that He . . . manifests His being, power, wisdom and life through His works and especially in the mind, will and personality of man. We believe that the mind of man reflects, though imperfectly, the mind of God, and we reject as a betrayal of human dignity all attempts to explain man in merely material terms.*

Would you agree with the statement? What good things do you see in it? Why would it be inadequate as a creed for you or your congregation? What Protestant denominations would probably be able to accept and use this as a creed?

For greater Los Angeles, 35 percent of respondents to a 1987 survey identified themselves as following Reform beliefs and practices. That figure is believed to be compatible with North American totals.

3. Conservative Judaism

Somewhere between the liberalism of Reform Judaism and the rigidity of Orthodox Judaism lies the traditional but updated form of Jewish expression called Conservative Judaism. Conservative Jews generally affirm the truth of the Hebrew Scriptures, teach Hebrew to their children, observe the traditional dietary laws and the festivals, and generally conform their lives to the requirements of the Torah. On the other hand, they make certain concessions to the modern world and modify some ancient laws to fit life today.

For example, Orthodox Jews will not ride in a car on the Sabbath because they believe it violates the prohibition against making a fire on the Sabbath. Some do not use an electric light switch on the Sabbath for the same reason—because of the spark that occurs when the switch is pulled. Conservative Jews, however, while they would probably avoid building a fire, would consider avoidance of a car an unnecessary rigidity. The numbers of Jewish people identifying themselves as Conservative total 33 percent in the Los Angeles survey.

As you look over the three forms of Judaism discussed above, what parallels in the Protestant community can you see? Could Christians be put into categories of orthodox, reform, and conservative?

4. Another Division—A Controversial One

Increasing numbers of Jews are becoming Christians while at the same time keeping their identity as Jews. Note that this is what Paul did (**Acts 22:3–21**). Some of these Jewish Christians prefer to be called fulfilled, completed, or messianic Jews. Some of these Jewish believers have formed congregations which call themselves messianic synagogues. Often these congregations are considered traitorous by the Jewish community— and are viewed with suspicion by the Christian community. What might be some advantages and disadvantages of such separate messianic syna- gogues for nurturing Jewish Christians in faith? for enabling them to witness to others? (See **1 Corinthians 9:19–23; Galatians 3:28.**)

Doctrine

Though there is agreement in the Jewish community on the *Shema,* much of what is affirmed about God—those things that come under the area of traditional theology—are left as open questions or are areas on which there is little common agreement. Though there is no formal Jewish creed, these generalizations would be true for most Jews. They affirm the following:

1. God is One. He lives and rules. He is involved in the world and human life.
2. God chooses and blesses His people. Jews are unique. (A Jew who becomes a baptized Christian is viewed at best as an apostate Jew but is usually considered to be a traitor and no longer a Jew.)

3. The primary purpose of life is to live ethically in relationship to God and in service to others.
4. Religion is primarily a way of living and not a collection of tenets to be believed and taught.
5. The family is the basic religious unit and the center of individual identity and strength.

What strengths—and what inadequacies—do you see in these statements? How do these affirmations demonstrate themselves in the lives and attitudes of Jewish people? How would a statement of common Christian attitudes be the same or different from these?

Movements within Judaism

Because of the emphasis in Judaism on this life and on the uniqueness and chosenness of the Jews as God's people, sometimes movements across Judaism are stronger than teachings.

1. *Messianism.* Though the waiting and watching for the coming of the Messiah was very strong in Judaism at times in the past, it is almost dormant now. Few contemporary Jews expect the Messiah to come now or that God is going to establish a world rule of peace under the Jewish Messiah. But the forward-looking hope that centered in the Messiah is still there. Many Jews still long for and work for peace and harmony in the world, so that "the wolf shall dwell with the lamb" (Isaiah 11:6) and all people can live together as brothers and sisters.
2. *Zionism.* The strong movement in Judaism today, finding expression in all forms of Judaism, is Zionism. It is the politico-religious movement to strengthen the nation of Israel in its home in Palestine. Many Jews are committed to the movement and invest large sums of time and money in the effort. Though seen as a fulfillment of scriptural promise by some and the salvation of the Jewish people's identity by others, most Jews at least see the establishment of modern Israel as a nation as an enrichment of Jewish life.

Are there any cross-denominational movements in the Christian church today that might parallel Messianism or Zionism? What forms do they take? What strengths or weaknesses are there in these kinds of religious movements?

Jewish Life Today

In the United States and Canada the life of the Jew is probably not significantly different from that of his or her Protestant or Catholic neighbor. Jews are subject to the same pressures of materialism and secularism that others are. For many Jews religion is as meaningless and unimportant as it is for many who call themselves Christian. Because of the cultural pressure to turn away from all spirituality and to center life on self, the greatest threat to the maintenance of Judaism as an identifiable religious or ethnic group is probably not persecution but apathy. The largest group of Jews in the United States and Canada is not Orthodox, Reform, or Conservative, but essentially nonreligious. Because the nonreligious Jew belongs to no synagogue and ignores many of the laws that would tend to maintain his or her Jewishness (for instance, marriage within the Jewish community), it may indeed be secularism that finally makes the Jews indistinguishable from other people.

But there is a strength in the Jewish heritage that militates against the disappearance of Judaism. Even in many secular Jewish homes the traditional festivals are observed. These ceremonial and religious rituals probably do more to maintain the Jewish identity than any other single factor. They not only inject a note of religion into nonreligious homes, but they call to mind the suffering and deliverance of the Jewish people in the past and celebrate the persistence and perseverance of Judaism for the future.

The Lutheran Task Force on Witnessing to Jewish People has prepared seven Bible studies on the major Jewish festivals. Included are Sukkoth, Yom Kippur, Hanukkah, Rosh Hashanah, Purim, Shavuoth, and Passover. To order these studies, contact the Board for Mission Services, LCMS, 1333 S. Kirkwood Road, St. Louis, MO 63122-7295, Attention: Chairman, Task Force on Witnessing to Jewish People.

Look back at lesson 2. What powerful affirmations about Jews and their strength and specialness can you find in the celebrations of Purim and Hanukkah? Why would these festivals tend to strengthen Jewish community? Do Christians have any celebrations that are similar?

Building Jewish Community

The following are other festivals that are observed in many Jewish homes today:

1. *Pesach* **(Passover).** Based on the deliverance of the Hebrews from Egypt as recorded in the first 12 chapters of Exodus. The Orthodox observance includes careful cleaning and preparation of the house and the use of special foods (kosher) and special utensils, culminating in the Seder meal. The Seder is like a worship service in the home that includes prayers, readings from the Bible, singing, and eating. Prescribed foods are ritually prepared, including unleavened bread, leg of lamb or roast fowl, wine, fruits, and nuts.

   Scan **Exodus 12.** What meaning does the festival have for Jews? Why are the special foods important? What does the festival say about Jewish uniqueness? What connections do you see with the Lord's Supper?

2. *Rosh Hashanah* **and** *Yom Kippur.* Rosh Hashanah is the beginning of the Jewish year and is observed with special services in the synagogue or temple at which Scripture passages like **Genesis 22** and **1 Samuel 1** are read. Since the theme of Rosh Hashanah is remembrance, what "rememberings" do you find in these portions of Scripture that make them appropriate for the beginning of the year?

   Rosh Hashanah begins the 10 days of "awe" or repentance before Yom Kippur—the Day of Atonement.

   What connection do you see in the tradition of beginning the year with repentance and the Christian custom of beginning the year with Advent?

   Yom Kippur is the holiest of days. It includes five special services of repentance and forgiveness. Scan the instructions for Yom Kippur in **Leviticus 16.** What parts of the ritual prescribed there would be difficult for modern Jews to carry out? What connection with Christianity do you see in the fact that the holiest of Jewish religious days has to do with repentance and forgiveness.

A major Christian festival is Good Friday, commemorating Christ's death on the cross. What does that event have to say about repentance and forgiveness? (See for example **Psalm 49:7; Romans 5:8; 1 Timothy 2:5; Ephesians 1:7.**) What differences are there between the Christian view of repentance and forgiveness and a modern Jewish view such as the following:

Repentance and atonement are integral parts of Judaism. It is within the power of every man to redeem himself from sin by resolutely breaking away from it and by repenting or returning to God. . . . This covenant is without the need of an intermediary or vicarious Savior. Judaism for its adherents is not unfulfilled, nor is it incomplete; indeed, there is no religious void which Jesus or any other like figure could fill (Rabbi A. James Rudin in Jewish Views of Jesus, *pp. 3–4).*

For Discussion

1. What was most significant (interesting, important) for you in this lesson? Why?
2. "Jews as a nation and religion will last forever." Agree? Why or why not?
3. What strengths in Jewish religion and religious observance do you see that could be learned by the Christian community?
4. What specific things can Jews and Christians do together to combat the materialism and secularism that result in an increasingly immoral, selfish, and violent society?

5. Salvation and the Jews

The Aim of This Session

1. To better understand and appreciate God's saving purpose for Jews and Gentiles as revealed in three key chapters of the Bible—**Romans 9–11.**
2. To adopt for ourselves the apostle's attitude: "My heart's desire and prayer to God for them [our Jewish neighbors] is that they may be saved" **(Romans 10:1).**

Procedure

Read the Bible passages section by section as each is identified in the subtitles of this lesson. Share responses to the questions listed. Also feel free to *ask* any questions about any verse or section you don't understand and to *share* your thoughts and feelings about what you read. Most important of all, ask and discuss this question: What is God saying to us (me) today in and through His Word?

Blessings Unlimited: Romans 9:1–5

1. **Verses 4–5** summarize God's great acts of salvation for Israel: Sonship—see **Hosea 11:1; Exodus 4:22–23.** Glory—**Exodus 40:34.** Covenants—remember lesson 1 of this course? What are some of the promises Israel received? Who are the patriarchs? Which greatest act of God for and through His people does **verse 5** point to? (Compare

NIV and KJV with RSV. NIV translates this verse most accurately.)
2. What is there in Paul's background that led him to such unceasing anguish for his fellow Jews? What in *our* background might well lead us to such concern?

God's Promise Stands Sure: 9:6–13

1. Not all the physical descendants of Abraham, Isaac, or Jacob (Israel) belong to Israel **(verse 6)**. What can this mean? Are there two kinds of Israel? Or more? If so, can you give them a name and describe them? (See **Romans 2:28–29; 4:9–12; Galatians 3:6–9**.)
2. What do these texts have to say to the person who claims, "Sure, I'm a child of God. I'm a member of the doctrinally pure church"? Or ". . . My father was a pastor"? Or ". . . I was raised in a Christian home"? Or ". . . I'm descended from Abraham"?

God's Mercy Has Purpose: 9:14–24

When God richly poured out His mercy on Israel **(Romans 9:4–5)**, He set into motion a plan, the ultimate goal of which was the salvation of the world **(Genesis 18:18; John 3:16)**. So here God's mercy and compassion **(verse 15)** underlie His judgment on Pharaoh and his judicial hardening of that proud king's heart. God's goal is nothing less than "that My name may be proclaimed in all the earth" **(verse 17; see Exodus 14:4)**. God uses His *power* to serve His saving purpose, His mercy.

After Pharaoh again and again hardened his own heart in the face of the plagues God sent on Egypt **(Exodus 8:15; 8:32)**, God's judgment fell on this obdurate enemy of His people. God's hardening of Pharaoh's heart is a chilling demonstration that God's patience can finally be exhausted, His wrath called down.

"One vessel for beauty and another for menial use" **(verse 21)**—for example, "a lovely vase, and . . . a pipe for sewage" (Phillips). Note that God calls out for Himself a chosen people from among Jews and Gentiles **(verse 24)**. God's patient enduring with "objects" that cry out to be destroyed—like Pharaoh—results in making known to people His love for His chosen ones **(verses 22–23)**. God's long-suffering through 10 plagues before His judgment fell on Pharaoh magnified in the eyes of the world His ultimate rescue of His people.

1. How did this same long-suffering of God work out for the ultimate good of Joseph and his family? (See **Genesis 50:15–21.**)
2. Out of evil, even the evil of persecution, God also today continues to work good for His elect. Read **Romans 8:28, 31–39.** What is our proof positive that He is working for our good? Can you give an example from your own life of God working good from evil?

The Record of History: 9:25–29

That believers shall be called and saved from both the Jews and the Gentiles **(verse 24)** is shown by prophecy and history. **Verses 25–26** (see also **Hosea 1:1–10)** show how God's saving purpose was worked out even in the 10 Israelite tribes that were taken into captivity, intermarried with Gentiles, and thus disappeared. Hearing the Gospel and coming to faith, some of the descendants of these disobedient people would once again be called "sons of the living God." Thus some of the "lost" 10 tribes would be saved.

Similarly, the text quoted from **Isaiah 10:22 (verse 27)** and **Isaiah 1:9 (verse 29)** emphasize that some—a remnant—from Israel will be saved.

Faith: The Key to Righteousness: 9:30–33

"Gentiles" **(verse 30)** here means the non-Jewish people of Paul's day, whose worship of pagan gods was often associated with immorality.

1. What law is meant in **verse 31?** How does **Romans 3:19–31** further explain why many in Israel did not attain righteousness, while some Gentiles did attain it. Is it because Gentiles were (or are) better than Jews? because the Law is no good?
2. Who or what is the "stone that will make men stumble" **(verse 33)?**

Christ, the Answer: Romans 10:1–13

1. What applications do you draw from **10:1** for today? for your own personal life? as a member of a Christian congregation?
2. In what sense is Christ the "end of the law" **(verse 4)?** (Scan **Romans 4** as you share responses.)

3. Salvation is only through faith in Christ—for Jew and Gentile alike. True or false? What reasons can you give for your answer? (Again also see **Romans 4.**)

The Gospel Call: 10:14–21

1. **Verses 14–18** depict the spreading to *all* people of the Good News about God's forgiveness. Who (or what) is the heart of the Good News (**verse 17**)? What is the result of the message (**verse 16–17**)?
2. **Verses 19–21** zero in on the Gospel's effect specifically on Israel. **Verse 19** quotes **Deuteronomy 32:21** with its imagery of a marriage relationship. God would make *Israel* jealous by reaching out in mercy to the Gentiles. What is God's ultimate goal in thus provoking Israel to jealousy? (Read **Deuteronomy 32:21–36,** especially **verse 36.**)

The Remnant: Romans 11:1–6

Refer back to **9:6–7.** What is another name for the remnant? See also **John 10:16.** What makes one a part of the remnant, a member of Christ's flock, a member of the church?

Israel/Gentiles: God's Plan: 11:7–12

1. Who were some of the elect (**verse 7**) during Jesus' life? See **Matthew 13:10–17; John 12:37–43.** Who are the elect today? How can one know whether he or she is part of the elect?
2. Parent: "Eat your nice dinner." Child: "I don't want it." Parent: "Okay, then I'll give it to your brother." Child: "No, it's mine! I want it." Share a time when you were in a situation like that child. Compare that kind of situation with **Romans 11:11–12** and **10:19.**

Roots and Branches: 11:13–24

Try to summarize the point and meaning of the parable of the olive tree. Who (or what) is (are) the cultivated olive tree? the root? the natural branches? the wild olive shoot? What is God telling us in these verses? What meaning does it have for your life?

The Mystery: 11:25–27

1. What is the mystery (**verse 25**)? See **Ephesians 1:9–10; 2:11–18; 3:1–6.** Remember that the mystery is something positive and good.
2. What is meant by "all Israel" (**verse 26**)? This is a difficult verse, and Bible scholars do not agree on its interpretation. Some think this means that every Jew who ever lived will be saved—sometime, somehow. Why can this not be the meaning (**verses 7–10, 25**)? Refer again to **9:6–8** (also **Romans 2:28–29**). If "all Israel" is not all the physical descendants of Abraham, who is meant by this verse?

Mercy upon All: 11:28–32

What reason do these verses give us to love one another and rejoice in God—regardless of whether we are of Jewish or Gentile physical descent?

Glory to God: 11:33–36

Look at this hymn of praise closely. Most likely you felt inadequate and maybe frustrated at times because these chapters are so hard to understand. But this is what mortals come up against when we want to understand the unfathomable mysteries of God. Yet in Christ we see His face—and know that His ultimate purpose is our good. So, for our salvation and for the salvation of Jews, we sing with St. Paul: "To Him be glory for ever. Amen."

6. *Evangelism and the Jews*

The Aim of This Session

1. To understand some of the reasons for the resistance of the Jews toward Christian evangelism.
2. To recognize our part in building barriers of mistrust and suspicion between Jew and Christian and to repent.
3. To reaffirm our commitment to be witnesses to the good news of salvation in Jesus Christ.
4. To rededicate ourselves to a mission of loving witness to individuals.

The Mulliganites Are Coming

A new religious sect has become popular where you live. This sect teaches that a new revelation has been received from God that finally and completely reveals the meaning of the New Testament. "It's not that Christianity is wrong," say the Mulliganites. "It's just that Christians don't have the finished truth that we have discovered. When they come to our church they will know the real truth."

The Mulliganites are aggressive missionaries. Many of your friends and neighbors convert. The Mulliganites subtly let it be known that they consider membership in their church good qualification for the best jobs and a prerequisite for membership in the best organizations. Meanwhile they would appreciate it if Christians would stay out of their neighborhoods, schools, and clubs. You live among the Mulliganites. Most of the time they don't mistreat you. They just ignore you.

Then, one fine day, the Mulliganites announce that they are starting a "new" crusade to convert all Christians to Mulliganism. The drive is announced in the paper and on TV. Notable Mulliganites are interviewed in the media.

Later you are standing on a corner in your hometown. A nice-looking man approaches. "I see by the cross you are wearing that you are a Christian," he says. "I want to talk to you about Mulliganism."

How would you respond? What would you say? How would you feel?

Of course the example is kind of silly—surely it could not happen. And too, it does not exactly parallel the relationship between Christians and Jews. But setting aside those deficiencies in the example, discuss your feelings and attitudes in that situation. What kinds of relationships would be established between you and your Mulliganite neighbors? What might be the final result? What parallels in the world today and in history do you see? How are they similar to or different from the Mulliganite example?

Pride and Prejudice

Much of the history of the world is a history of injustice and hatred between peoples. In the name of nationality Greeks have hated Turks, Koreans have hated Japanese, and Saxons have hated Normans—and the list could go on endlessly. In the name of religion Christians have persecuted heretics, Muslims have converted peoples by the sword, and Protestants have oppressed Catholics—and again the list could go on and on.

Through the centuries, the relationship between Christians and Jews has been deplorable. The persecutions carried out against Jews by people who were Christian in name or from "Christian" nations are a terrible embarrassment to all Christians.

Though recent years have seen notable efforts to improve Jewish/non-Jewish relations and though Jews live in an atmosphere of general freedom and acceptance in the United States and Canada, the relationship between the two communities has not been good. The prejudice, bitterness, and antagonism of centuries die slowly.

The problem is that, in our sinfulness, bad feelings and attitudes feed on themselves and seem to multiply over time rather than die. That truth is surely demonstrated in the way Jews and Christians have related and still relate to one another today.

On the one hand, the very struggle to survive in a hostile world has contributed to the character of modern Jews and their community. Jews cling to their identity as Jews. They pride themselves in their heritage and their place as God's chosen. Like anyone else, they strive to succeed. They form close internal ties to one another. Many tend to mistrust those outside of their own people—and with good historical reason, as we have seen.

But their separation and internalization—and their striving for excellence—are misinterpreted by many who see not strength and healthy pride, but arrogance. And that pictured arrogance engenders more negative feeling. The non-Jew who has not yet overcome his or her prejudice against Jews is reinforced in that prejudice when confronted by their separation or striving. And the Jew, who out of fear avoids the non-Jew, sees only angry prejudice in response to his or her anxiety.

The cycle of pride feeding prejudice and prejudice feeding fear continues—so the hatred and persecution continue. If we are seriously going to talk about ministering to the Jews or witnessing to them, it is that cycle of antagonism, bitterness, and hatred that is going to have to be broken before anything but more bad feeling and fear can be produced. Suspicion breeds suspicion. Fear breeds fear. Only real, genuine, God-given love can overcome fear. "Perfect love casts out fear," wrote John (**1 John 4:18**). Nothing else.

What Do We Do Now?

Repent. A good place to start in any religious endeavor is with repentance—and that is particularly true in this case. Unless we are willing to look honestly at our own feelings of pride and prejudice against the Jews, and unless we are willing to sincerely repent and seek God's forgiveness in Jesus Christ, there is little chance we will ever do anything other than feed the fires of suspicion and fear in our relationship to the Jews.

We need to ask questions like these:

How often have I assumed I could categorize or predict a person's attitude or behavior simply because he or she was a Jew?

How often have I undertaken evangelism to the Jews or anyone else because of my need to speak instead of their need to hear?

How often have I fostered feelings of separation, hatred, and fear?

How often have I tried to witness to a Jew or another person without listening—treating the person as an object of my "sales pitch" for the Good News, without ever knowing the person's name and needs?

Have I ever discriminated against a Jewish friend or neighbor by not sharing with him or her what Jesus means to me because I feared getting into an argument? (**1 Peter 3:15** speaks to that!)

What other questions can we ask ourselves that will reveal our common weakness and sinfulness even as we try to go about the Lord's work?

What is the solution as we repent? Where must we go? No one needs the good news of salvation and forgiveness in Jesus Christ more than we do.

Understand. If we want to make progress in changing attitudes toward Jews and breaking the cycle of pride and prejudice, we need to understand what it means to be a Jew today. But that understanding will have to be more than head knowledge. We can understand how the sun has spots and how a clock works by reading or observation, but we cannot walk in other people's shoes, feel their feelings, or accept them as persons until we have been there.

We can study Jews in courses like this one and even recreate some of the experiences of the Jews by little exercises like the one that began this lesson. But that is still only partial understanding.

There needs to be a real attempt to bridge the bad feelings and the prejudices and reach out to the Jews in love—as individuals. Until we have entered the experience of a Jewish friend and lived through a crisis with him or her, until we have spent the time and emotional energy necessary to hear his or her needs, pains, hopes, and dreams, we will not even come close to understanding.

Read **Romans 12:9–21.** What is commanded here? List the positive words. Make a list of specific things you can do as individuals and as a group to relate in positive ways to Jewish people around you. Talk about how you will respond if you meet suspicion on their part. What specific things in your community can you and your Jewish neighbors do together? What experiences can you share? What opportunities to talk as equals can you help to create? What chances for mutual caring can you get under way? If we cannot come up with honest answers to these questions and specific plans for action, we will not be able to move to our next step—our witness.

What about Our Witness?

Without apology, as committed Christians we believe "all have sinned and fall short of the glory of God" **(Romans 3:23)** and that "He died for all" **(2 Corinthians 5:15)**. Without apology we can say with Paul, "I am not ashamed of the gospel: it is the power of God for salvation to every one who has faith, to the Jew first and also to the Greek [Gentile]" **(Romans 1:16)**.

But having said that, we are not suddenly given license to accost people; to oppress them with our witness; to threaten them; to treat them as objects for our endeavors; to consider them inferior; or to invade their lives, feelings, and homes with our need to speak.

Here is a partial list of "rules" for witnessing to Jews or anyone else for that matter:

1. *Witness is to persons—not groups.* When we speak of our Savior, we need to know that we are talking to a unique person with individual needs. The Gospel is the good news that the Savior touches hearts and lives where those hearts and lives need His healing presence. (Note Jesus' infinite patience and very personal approach to one woman in **John 4.**)

2. *Witness is listening.* If we do not take the time to listen to a person's name and needs, how can we share the Good News?

3. *Witness is loving.* It imitates Jesus with Zacchaeus or with the blind man (see **Luke 19:1–10** and **John 9:1–7**). It takes the time to go to a house for a visit as a friend or to bend over in the dust to make a healing paste to put on one man's eyes. What does it say to the person we are witnessing to if our Good News, our "love," is only in our mouths? What does **1 John 3:18** say about that kind of love? What does Jesus say is the mark of His disciples (**John 13:35**)? What do these passages mean for our evangelism?

4. *Witness is sharing.* We must be as willing to hear about the faith of the person we are witnessing to as we are willing to tell about our own. How else can trust be established?

5. *Witness is giving.* We need to remember that the Gospel is good news

and *God's* gift. Faith is a work of the Spirit and not of ours. We do not create faith in another person by the power of our persuasion, the aggressiveness of our approach, or the brilliance of our argumentation. We preach Jesus Christ. Paul said, "I decided to know nothing among you except Jesus Christ and Him crucified" **(1 Corinthians 2:2).** What does that passage mean for our evangelism?

Complete the list yourself. What other ideas, cautions, reminders, encouragement, and guidelines do we need as we undertake our task as witnesses to the Gospel of Jesus Christ—to the Jew or to anyone?

The Task Force on Witnessing to Jewish People has been established to serve the cause of reaching the lost sheep of Israel with the Good News that Y'shua (the Jewish way to say Jesus) is the promised Messiah of Israel. Since 1974, this task force has developed many useful materials to prepare people for Jewish evangelism. One audiocassette series, Beginning from Jerusalem, helps the listener learn more about Jewish people, their backgrounds, and how to present the Gospel in a loving, yet direct manner. There are also filmstrips and videos that inform people of some of the ways to reach out. And for those who want a hands-on experience, there is the Apple of His Eye outreach, which takes place in the summertime in New York City. It is a two-week adventure in evangelism and a chance for people to learn while doing. If you would like information about any of the above, write to the Task Force on Witnessing to Jewish People, Board for Mission Services, LCMS, 1333 S. Kirkwood Road, St. Louis, MO 63122-7295.

For Further Discussion

1. What was most significant (interesting, important) for you in this lesson? Why?
2. It is your task to design a plan to improve Jewish-Christian relationships in your community. What could you do? How many of those proposals can you carry out?
3. Select one member of your class to be a Jewish person visiting your Bible class. You want to present the Gospel to him or her. Talk with and listen to your visiting "Jewish" friend. Then ask how he or she feels. What did you say that hurt? that helped? What approach might you have better used?

Glossary

Am B'ne Israel. See also B'nai B'rith. Literally, "people of the sons (or descendants) of Israel (or Jacob)." A collective term for Jews.

Babylonian exile. In 605 and 597 B.C. the Babylonian king Nebuchadnezzar carried into exile a number of residents of Judah. In 586 Nebuchadnezzar captured Jerusalem and ordered the temple destroyed. In 538 after capturing Babylon, the Persian king Cyrus issued an edict, allowing residents of Judah to return to their homeland and rebuild their temple. Some people did so in several groups over the span of about 100 years. The last group to return did so in 432 under Nehemiah.

B'nai B'rith. Oddly, this is not an Old Testament term, but it does occur in the New Testament. Literally it means "sons (or people) of the covenant (of circumcision)." The modern Jewish Anti-Defamation League is part of the B'nai B'rith organization.

Covenant. A promise or agreement entered into between two or more parties. In the Bible, covenants between God and people were initiated by God. God made a promise, sometimes gave a sign, and required people to uphold their end of the promise. E.g., God made a covenant with Abraham and his descendants. He promised to make of them a great nation, give them the land of Canaan, and be their God. The sign was the circumcision of all male children. Abraham's descendants were to be faithful to God.

Diaspora. A spreading out, a dispersion. Specifically in relation to Jews, the phenomenon since the *Babylonian exile* that generally more Jews have lived outside Palestine than inside Palestine.

Gemara. Records and minutes of the case discussions and legal debates conducted by rabbis as they interpreted the Mishnah.

Ghetto. A part of a city (usually walled off) where Jews were forced to live by themselves.

Hellenism. The use of Greek ideas, Greek culture, and Greek language. Beginning at the time of Alexander the Great (who ruled from 336– 323 B.C.), it spread throughout the Mediterranean world. Its pagan philosophy and proponents were a threat to pious Jews and to Judaism in Palestine, especially in the second century before Christ.

Holocaust. This literally means "a whole burnt offering," and it applied originally to Jewish sacrifices. In modern times *the Holocaust* refers to the Nazis' systematic murdering of nearly six million European Jews.

Jahveh. See *Yahweh.*

Midrash. An exegesis or explanation of a text, especially a biblical text.

Mishnah. The oral law, as contrasted with the written Law, the Pentateuch. It is somewhat an explanation of parts of the Pentateuch (the first five books of the Bible). The Mishnah is essentially the "tradition of the elders" mentioned in the New Testament **(Mark 7:5).** The Mishnah was codified by "the rabbi," Judah ha-Nasi, about 200 A.D.

Pogrom. An organized riot, usually designed and executed by Christian rulers, to destroy all or part of certain Jewish communities.

Talmud. The large body of rabbinic learning comprising the Mishnah and the Gemara, relating to all kinds of Jewish life and practice. There are two Talmuds, the Palestinian and the Babylonian, of which the latter is the more complete and authoritative.

Tanak. An acronym symbolizing the three main parts of the Hebrew Bible.
T stands for Torah, the Pentateuch;
N stands for Neviim, the Prophets;
K stands for Kethuvim, the (other) Writings.
Christians refer to the Tanak as "the Old Testament."

Yahweh. This is the distinctive and peculiar name for the God of Israel, revealed to Moses in **Exodus 3:14–15** and **6:3.** The heathen spoke of and acknowledged gods, but to Israel Yahweh was the one true God.

DUE